The Hidden Treasures
FOUND IN THE BIBLE

CHRYSTAL V. HOLLINS

The Hidden Treasures Found in the Bible

Copyright © 2021 by Chrystal V. Hollins. All rights reserved.

No part of this publication may be reproduced, stored in a retrieval system or transmitted in any way by any means, electronic, mechanical, photocopy, recording or otherwise without the prior permission of the author except as provided by USA copyright law.

The opinions expressed by the author are not necessarily those of URLink Print and Media.

1603 Capitol Ave., Suite 310 Cheyenne, Wyoming USA 82001
1-888-980-6523 | admin@urlinkpublishing.com

URLink Print and Media is committed to excellence in the publishing industry.

Book design copyright © 2021 by URLink Print and Media. All rights reserved.

Published in the United States of America

Library of Congress Control Number: 2021912031
ISBN 978-1-64753-835-4 (Paperback)
ISBN 978-1-64753-836-1 (Digital)

06.04.21

TABLE OF CONTENTS

Prologue v

Day 1: Abundance 1
St. Luke 6:45

Day 2: Burden 3
Galatians 6:2

Day 3: Communion 6
1 Corinthians 10:16

Day 4: Deny 8
St. Matthew 16:24

Day 5: Eternal 10
Romans 6:23

Day 6: Faith 12
Galatians 2:20

Day 7: Gift 14
James 1:17

Day 8: Husband 16
Proverbs 18:22

Day 9: Intercession 18
Romans 8:26

Day 10: Jehovah 20
Isaiah 12:2

Day 11: Kingdom 22
St. Matthew 6:33

Day 12: Leaven 24
    1 Corinthians 5:7

Day 13: Marriage 26
    Hebrews 13:4

Day 14: Oath 28
    Numbers 30:2

Day 15: Prudent 30
    Proverbs 12:23

Day 16: Quarrel 32
    St. Luke 17:3

Day 17: Repent 34
    2 Peter 3:9

Day 18: Savior 36
    1 Timothy 4:10

Day 19: Testimony 38
    Psalm 71:16

Day 20: Unjust 40
    2 Timothy 2:15

Day 21: Vain 42
    Psalm 127:1

Day 22: Worship 44
    Psalm 95:1

Day 23: Youth 46
    1 Timothy 4:12

Day 24: Zeal 48
    Psalm 71:23

Epilogue 51

PROLOGUE

The Bible has many words, phrases, content, and insight. One could open the Bible and stumble upon a word or phrase within a passage or Scripture verse that speaks volume in their life and current condition or situation. God is a wonder and one of many mysteries. While reading this book, I will like to share with you all the gems that are in the Bible that can shape and transform the mind and the heart. So, welcome to the treasure chest of inspiration.

DAY 1

ABUNDANCE

READING: St. Luke 6:45

To begin, what is *abundance* or an *abundant life*? Many may look at this word or phrase and think of increase, plenty of (not any lack), strength, power, completion, and even riches. The responses are true and the answers are correct. Therefore, the word *abundance* or the phrase an *abundant life* can be defined using all the examples above, but how does the Bible define abundance?

According to Luke 6:45, " a good man out of the good treasure of his heart bringeth forth that which is good; and an evil man out of the evil treasure of his heart bringeth forth that which is evil: for of the abundance of the heart his mouth speaketh" (KJV). Whatever is stored in the heart rather good or evil, reaps that of the same fruit. So if a person has good intentions, right morals, and pureness of heart than those seeds will reap that of good fruit. But if a person has bad intentions, wrong morals, and impurity in their heart than those seeds will reap that of bad fruit.

Prayer: *Heavenly Father,*

Let our life experience the unlimited gift of increase and success. AMEN

<u>Reflection</u>- Why is loving your enemies and examining the heart of a good man important in the world today?

DAY 2

BURDEN

READING: Galatians 6:2

Next, is the word *burden*. What definition comes to mind when this word enters one thought? One may think of this phrase as negative, sorrows, obstacles, struggles, and hardships. But what if I were to say that the word *burden* is actually a good thing. The first thought that may come to mind is Chrystal, you are crazy to even think that. However, it is true.

For the Apostle Paul defines burden as a motivator and an action, "bear ye one another's burdens and so fulfill the law of Christ" (Gal. 6:2, KJV). So what does Paul mean? Paul states that one's burden should not be handled alone but with the aid of another; the assistance of a friend or a family member. In other words, Paul says do not struggle with a burden alone and do not seek any help or comfort from your fellow man or friend.

Instead invite or welcome another to cry and mourn with you or speak life and deliverance to that situation, which shows the burden being used as a motivator. When a person experiences heaviness or pressed motion that fills up in the heart and/ or in the Spirit. The reason why a person feels that heaviness is because God is pressing on others what is pressed or place in His heart and in His Spirit.

The burden or burdens that a person feels can be an unexplainable sadness or pity for other people or making a severe sacrifice to express the amount of love that someone has for another.

-Calvary-

These examples friend are two that I personally experienced in life, but with God's help I found the strength I need to endure and make it. This same power help others as well.

Prayer: *Heavenly Father,*

Help us to embrace the growth of maturity within the burdens one faces. AMEN

Reflection- How can one show justification by carrying another's burden?

_____
_____
_____
_____
_____
_____
_____
_____
_____
_____
_____
_____
_____
_____
_____
_____
_____
_____
_____
_____
_____
_____
_____
_____
_____
_____
_____
_____

DAY 3

COMMUNION

READING: 1 Corinthians 10:16

Now for this phrase *Communion* two scripture verses are used to fully express the importance of His burial. So what is the true meaning of Communion? Why does one engage or participate? The answer is within the scripture verse 1 Cor. 10:16, "the cup of blessing which we bless, is it not the communion of the blood of Christ? The bread which we break, is it not the communion of the body of Christ?" (KJV).

The drinking of the wine which signifies the blood of Jesus Christ welcomes one to partake in His suffering while the eating of the bread which signifies the bones of Jesus Christ, welcomes one to His death; the killing of His body. Following this verse is another scripture that speaks of the importance of unity. According to 2 Cor. 6:14, "be ye not unequally yoked together with unbelievers: for what fellowship hath righteousness with unrighteousness? and what communion hath light with darkness?" (KJV).

In this verse, Paul states not to become mingled and associated with relations of this world. Being as a light into this dark world, let one righteous life lure others into seeking a relationship with Christ. So ask yourself this question, "Will I let my light shine?"

Prayer: *Heavenly Father,*

Please remind us of the blood-shed and the body broken for our wickedness. AMEN

<u>Reflection</u>- If you were to write a letter to a church regarding Communion what would you say?

_____
_____
_____
_____
_____
_____
_____
_____
_____
_____
_____
_____
_____
_____
_____
_____
_____
_____
_____
_____
_____
_____

DAY 4

DENY

READING: St. Matthew 16:24

In the Bible, the word *deny* means to put aside or away permanently. When one decides to follow Jesus Christ and surrender their life to Him, the denial of the body which the Word defines as the **flesh** is given to Christ. Based on St. Matthew 16:24, "then said Jesus unto his disciples, if any man will come after me, let him deny himself and take up his cross, and follow me" (KJV).

In this verse, Jesus tells the twelve disciples that one cannot follow him while dwelling in their flesh (one's selfish desires and ambition). They will have to deny self (put aside or away permanently) to follow Jesus with their whole heart. In other words, a person will need a heart of commitment and obedience. In which is not impossible to receive and gain.

Any person that wants to follow Christ must seek Him in Spirit and in truth said John in the book of St. John chapter 4:24. God is the Father and Jesus Christ is the Son. So if one seeks the Father they will have to seek the Son and if one seeks the Son then they will have to seek the Father.

Prayer: *Heavenly Father,*

Put away our fleshy ways and desires that we may be more like Thee.
AMEN

<u>Reflection</u>- What does deny, take up the cross, and follow me really means?

_____
_____
_____
_____
_____
_____
_____
_____
_____
_____
_____
_____
_____
_____
_____
_____
_____
_____
_____
_____
_____
_____
_____

DAY 5

ETERNAL

READING: Romans 6:23

Being a term or word use as ever-lasting and a long time, the meaning carries a heavy weight behind it. True, the word eternal does mean ever-lasting, a long period of time, and forever but the question is *where* will one spend this eternal time at? Where or what will be the final destination (place) that the soul may find rest after existing a physical life? What a good question.

There is an answer found in the book of Romans 6:23, "For the wages of sin is death; but the gift of God is eternal life through Jesus Christ our Lord" (KJV). In this scripture, the Apostle Paul speaks to the Church of Rome about the result of sin versus the result of life. When one think of wages, the idea of work and money comes to mind because this word 'wage' is a noun that means money given or received for work or some type of service. But in this verse, a person doesn't get money for committing their sin, but death both physical (literal) and spiritual.

It is true, however, that a result will come from the practice of sin most likely bad. Yet, one could repent (ask for forgiveness and not do it anymore) and receive the gift (giving and something that doesn't have to be return) of life, not just physically but also spiritually. This is the result that the Apostle Paul wanted for the people of Rome and one that Jesus Christ wants for everyone.

Prayer: *Heavenly Father,*

Through Paul's words help us to receive and gain this eternal life. AMEN

Reflection- Can you think of a time when a wrong act led to destruction?

_____
_____
_____
_____
_____
_____
_____
_____
_____
_____
_____
_____
_____
_____
_____
_____
_____
_____
_____

DAY 6

FAITH

READING: Galatians 2:20

To have faith is to believe in the impossible and accept the unexplainable. The idea of a Spirit (God) recreating Himself to become a flesh with sinless motives and characteristics is impossible. The very thought of a physical man (Jesus) dying on a wooden tree known as a cross and three days later come back to life as if He were here all along is unexplainable. However, to be able to have an opportunity to seek God and have a relationship with Him which is free of charge takes faith.

Faith is what the Apostle Paul speaks of that is free and eternal. Apostle Paul says, "I am crucified with Christ: nevertheless I live; yet not I, but Christ liveth in me: and the life which I now live in the flesh I live by the faith of the Son of God, who loved me, and gave himself for me" (Gal. 2:20, KJV). In other words, since Paul denied himself to gain life through Jesus and live, what is the similar action that one should do to gain life for themselves? One will first have to believe in Christ in order to obey Him in which the faith is found in the believing or belief.

Then the next step will be to deny self (review chapter four for more details) and experience life through the love of Jesus Christ, so believe, deny, and experience the compassion of Jesus Christ.

Prayer: *Heavenly Father,*

We pray you enhance our faith in thee and trust more in you. AMEN

<u>Reflection</u>- How can someone be crucified with Christ yet live by faith?

DAY 7

GIFT

READING: James 1:17

When the Bible speaks of a gift, it usually refers to a special act of kindness or one that is not refundable. This gift can only be given by a giver whose kindness is unchangeable and the reward cannot be returned. This gift that is mention comes from a gentle delight of love found in the inner parts of men--the heart, which only God could give. According to James 1:17, "every good gift and every perfect gift is from above and cometh down from the Father of lights with whom is no variableness, neither shadow of turning" (KJV).

In other words, only God the Father can give out blessings that are both good (physically) and perfect (spiritually) to anyone who wants to receive them. Now in regards to the words…"whom is no variableness, neither shadow of turning." This means that the gift or gifts (plural) that God gives out doesn't change or vary. These gifts that God has are not fickle; here one moment then gone the next. His gifts are consistent and good.

Also, the gift(s) are not returnable or bad. Therefore, one doesn't have to worry about the gifts, which are the blessings that God provides being withheld or given back to the Father which is God.

Prayer: *Heavenly Father,*

We thank you for the perfect gifts and blessings that you provide and give. AMEN

Reflection- What are some good and perfect gifts that God has given you?

_____
_____
_____
_____
_____
_____
_____
_____
_____
_____
_____
_____
_____
_____
_____
_____
_____
_____
_____
_____

DAY 8

HUSBAND

READING: Proverbs 18:22

What makes a man a husband or husband material? A man that is the primitive example of one that follows the fruit of the Spirit. A man that has love (unconditional, emotional, physical, and spiritual) for his mate, joy (delight and gladness) in their mate, and peace (internal as well as external with himself and others). He has to practice the act of longsuffering (sticks it out when it gets tough, not easily shaken or moved, dedicated and faithful), and patience which is the same as gentleness.

He is an overall decent person with right moral conduct and one with much faith. These fruits of the Spirit can be found in the book of Galatians 5:22. A husband is not created but shaped and molded by the hands of God. He is also a leader and the pursuer. Based on the words of King Solomon, "whoso findeth a wife findeth a good thing, and obtaineth favour of the Lord" Proverbs 18:22 (KJV).

This means that whoever the man may be: tall, short, rich or poor and even intelligent or illiterate, if he seeks and finds a woman that he decides to marry that carries the same attributes that were mention prior to describe a man being a husband, than he is a blessed man and one that is favored by God. The favor comes from being privileged and receiving a special blessing from God which would be the lovely wife.

Prayer: *Heavenly Father,*

We thank you for the incredible husband or man that are in one's life. AMEN

Reflection- Why is finding a wife a good thing in a confused world?

___
___
___
___
___
___
___
___
___
___
___
___
___
___
___
___
___
___
___
___
___

DAY 9

INTERCESSION

READING: Romans 8:26

If one observes the word *intercession* carefully, the prefix pretty much says it all. To intercede is to come in between two and combine or mend what cannot be done on its own. In other words, it is to plea on another's behalf. So for Jesus Christ to intercede for men, he brought together two existent Spirits which are God and men. According to the letter that the Apostle Paul writes in Romans 8:26, "likewise the Spirit also helpeth our infirmities: for we know now what we should pray as we ought: but the Spirit itself maketh intercession for us with groanings which cannot be uttered" (KJV).

Therefore, Christ being both flesh and Spirit shed his blood for us, so that we could have a relationship with God. Through the death of Christ, the gap between God and people is mended; the distance that sin so greatly caused. Similar to Christ interceding for us, the Spirit known as the Holy Spirit intercedes within us when a person cannot seem to speak or cry out what is deep inside. In other words, the Spirit works on the person's behalf and is in tune with God's Spirit and will. It is through the Spirit that is inside and within us that reaches the depth of one's soul which reveals the desires of our heart and agony.

Prayer: *Heavenly Father,*

We are so grateful for the intercession that you made for us.

<u>Reflection</u>- Do you think it's possible to intercede (petition) for a lost soul?

DAY 10

JEHOVAH

READING: Isaiah 12:2

What does the word *Jehovah* stands for? What does it really mean? To answer this question, one will have to experience the existing power and might from God in which is given through His Son Jesus Christ. The true meaning behind the word or better yet the name of Jehovah can be found from a prophet who has experienced the power and might from God. In the book of Isaiah 12:2, the prophet states the answer.

"Behold, God is my salvation; I will trust, and not be afraid: for the Lord **Jehovah** is my strength and my song; he also is become my salvation" (KJV). Out of all the names that one may use to describe or call God, this one reveals the might and power that God possesses. The prophet Isaiah starts off by saying that *God is my salvation*, this means a protector and keeper; one that provides safety. Next, he says *I will trust and not be afraid*.

This means to rely and depend on whole-heartedly and not be fearful of anything. The prophet Isaiah calls God by a name that means 'strong' Jehovah and states how God is his strength and words of melody [my song] and again back to the beginning, God being his protector.

Prayer: *Heavenly Father,*

Your name is higher than any other name! AMEN

Reflection- What does the word *Jehovah* means to you?

_____
_____
_____
_____
_____
_____
_____
_____
_____
_____
_____
_____
_____
_____
_____
_____
_____
_____
_____
_____
_____
_____
_____
_____
_____

DAY 11

KINGDOM

READING: St. Matthew 6:33

If one really wants to inherit or gain the riches and abundant blessings of God, Matthew a disciple who was apart of Jesus's three and a half year ministry on earth, reveals how to get access to that. Before one seek their possession, family, career and etc. Why not seek something more that is worth one's time. Perhaps, the throne better known as the kingdom, "but seek ye first the kingdom of God, and his righteousness; and all these things shall be added unto you" (KJV). St. Matthew 6:33 will be a huge benefit for you.

When it came to seeking the kingdom first, Matthew a former tax collector learned about the throne by giving up all that he had to follow Jesus. By leading of example, he sought the kingdom when he sought Jesus first. Along with Jesus came his righteousness, which was everything that he desired. When one seeks Jesus first, they cannot help but to seek or find the good that comes with Him. He is a wonder and a friend that sticks closer than anyone. He offers great peace and rest to those who are in need of restoration and being rejuvenated.

Prayer: *Heavenly Father,*

We come to thank you for your love and access to the kingdom. AMEN

Reflection- When it speaks of the kingdom of God, what thought comes to mind?

_____
_____
_____
_____
_____
_____
_____
_____
_____
_____
_____
_____
_____
_____
_____
_____
_____
_____
_____
_____
_____
_____
_____
_____

DAY 12

LEAVEN

READING: 1 Corinthians 5:7

What does the word *leaven* mean? When a person thinks of this word, perhaps the idea of yeast in dough which is the raw ingredient of bread comes to mind or the thought of a sacrifice; a ceremonial event that represents the purity of one's body and soul. In accordance to this text, leaven signifies the old and unclean that must be removed. When the Apostle Paul heard of the report of fornication, he command that all the people cleanse themselves from this sin, "purge out therefore the old leaven, that ye may be a new lump, as ye are unleavened. For even Christ our passover is sacrificed for us" (1 Cor. 5:7, KJV).

Paul states that the sinful act(s) are a part of the nature of people. Thus, purging out this act will take some time and practice. In addition, to the purging of the sinful nature comes that of cleansing and pureness of mind, body, and Spirit. This is the cleansing that all believers need today. One that replenishes and restores the lack that sin blindly takes away.

Prayer: *Heavenly Father,*

Please remind us your holiness and pureness daily. AMEN

Reflection- What should one purge out or remove in their life?

DAY 13

MARRIAGE

READING: Hebrews 13:4

To seek a Holy God is to seek a holy and righteous relationship. This method of purity is implied to all things especially the bedroom. Therefore, the purity of a relationship can be found between the union of a couple. When it comes to the term 'marriage' or 'matrimony' the experience can either be exciting or scary depending on the chosen individuals. But the overall experience is memorable and one that God respects and honors.

According to Hebrews 13:4, "marriage is honorable in all, and the bed undefiled: but whoremongers and adulterers God will judge" (KJV). This verse demonstrates the proper conduct behavior that represents decency and order. The decency is found in the format of an union, while the order is found in the structure of an union. Marriage is a covenant. It is more than just a man and woman coming together but a promise.

One that is made before men as well as God and the hosts of angels. Therefore, marriage is not a matter that should be taken lightly, but one that two individuals are ready to commit to and abide in.

Prayer: *Heavenly Father,*

Let this honorable act of love be evidence of holy matrimony.

Reflection- Is it possible to pursue the act of marriage in life today?

_____

DAY 14

OATH

READING: Numbers 30:2

An oath is similar to that of a vow. It is a promise or a sworn behavior. A behavior that should come from the heart, directly from the heart. So when it comes to making an oath to God, one makes a promise that comes from the heart. Therefore, "if a man vow a vow unto the Lord, or swear an oath to bind his soul with a bond; he shall not break his word, he shall do according to all that proceedeth out of his mouth" (Num. 30:2, KJV).

Understanding and knowing that God keeps all of His promises should in a sense encourage the orator to keep theirs or at least try to. That's why it is important to be careful to what one says and promises. This verse is so prominent and reflective to a believer's relationship with God. The prominence comes from the well-known and noticeable, while the reflection shows how believers should be receptive.

To be prominent is to stand out and to reflect is to examine internally and change what must be externally. Therefore, if one makes a vow and or an oath to God ask Him for help and persistence to hold on and keep the word or words that comes from the mouth.

Prayer: *Heavenly Father,*

If one makes a vow (a promise) to God please help them to keep it. AMEN

Reflection- Do you think a promise made to God is greater or the same as any other promises? Why?

DAY 15

PRUDENT

READING: Proverbs 12:23

What does it mean to be prudent? Prudent or prudence can be the reserve insight or knowledge (understanding) of information. In other words, prudence identifies with that of meekness and being humble. So to be a prudent person, one will have to be wise and sober; not engaging in all and everything. Hence, "a prudent man concealeth knowledge: but the heart of fools proclaimeth foolishness" (Prov. 12: 23, KJV).

To conceal something is to hide or keep secretive; being quiet and not disclosing information, while the foolish does the complete opposite. The foolish will expose all and everything. They are very loud and tell all information. So when it comes to a person concealing knowledge, that individual doesn't divulge or participate in what goes on around them. But inside the heart of a foolish person comes that of paltry and lack of sense.

Therefore, if anyone decides or chooses to be a person with wisdom let him or her be prudent.

Prayer: *Heavenly Father,*

Let it be your will that we're wise and prudent. AMEN

Reflection- How can a person obtain the knowledge of a prudent man?

_____
_____
_____
_____
_____
_____
_____
_____
_____
_____
_____
_____
_____
_____
_____
_____
_____
_____
_____
_____
_____
_____
_____
_____

DAY 16

QUARREL

READING: St. Luke 17:3

Living in a world and society where many do what they want and when they want, to find amends especially between two individuals can be the most difficult and challenging act to do. Why is that? How come getting along with one another is so hard to do? The answer: because this is a world where many do what they want and when they want, but for some odd reason, people will not cooperate or forgive, which can be more dangerous than anything else.

So an answer is given to all if one chooses to apply this divine truth into their life. According to Luke, a person who observed and notated the life of Jesus. When it comes to quarreling, disagreements, and strife, Luke said, "take heed to yourselves: if thy brother trespass against thee, rebuke him; and if he repent, forgive him" (St. Luke 17:3, KJV). When Luke said these words, he was talking about being careful with one actions. We all know our own actions, but reactions can be unpredictable.

We know that when faced with obstacles and pressure one may respond so quickly that much thought didn't occur or do otherwise. That's why Luke state to take heed of yourselves--before reacting stop and think of what to do. Next, he said if someone wrongs you or another correct them and if they apologize forgive them. For this is how quarreling will cease and peace will arise.

Prayer: *Heavenly Father,*

Any bickering or issues that we may have with others please remove from our lives. AMEN

Reflection- Why is it important to correct or criticize a person who has wrong you?

_____
_____
_____
_____
_____
_____
_____
_____
_____
_____
_____
_____
_____
_____
_____
_____
_____

DAY 17

REPENT

READING: 2 Peter 3:9

To repent is to be extremely sorry for an action that has hurt someone. Repentance can demolish a heavy weight of guilty conscienceness that sits on a person's heart. It allows one to express how they feel and the opportunity to change one's life style. With repentance comes patience and this patience comes from God for, "the Lord is not slack concerning his promise, as some men count slackness; but is long-suffering to us-ward, not willing that any should perish but that all should come to repentance" (2 Peter 3:9, KJV).

This scripture is amazing. Peter explains so vividly how God's patience exceeds the length of time. God is not in a rush to destroy the world or the people in it, but desires that all will come to Him and build a relationship with Him before one dies and miss out on *all* the opportunities that God has for them. Now tell me who wouldn't want to serve a God like that? Who loves unconditionally and whose mercies endures forever!

Prayer: *Heavenly Father,*

Thank you Lord for your patience and love for us all. AMEN

Reflection- Why do you think God patiently waits until all repents?

DAY 18

SAVIOR

READING: 1 Timothy 4:10

When it comes to saving our Father above fits the description perfectly. A savior is someone that saves others from harm and danger. An example of a savior will be one who rescues and delivers from something much greater than what one expects. Like death, perhaps. When God a Spirit, incarnated Himself he was given a bodily form to save the world from turmoil and spiritual lack, "for therefore we both labour and suffer reproach, because we trust in the living God, who is the savior of all men, specially of those that believe" (1 Tim. 4:10, KJV).

We as believers endure the trials and obstacles that may come our way. The saints endure because Christ Jesus endured and is there to save and correct us. He is there to guide and protect us. He is there because Jesus Christ saves and loves.

Prayer: *Heavenly Father,*

Thank you for being our Savior and friend. AMEN

<u>Reflection</u>- If you had to describe an ideal Savior what would you say?

_____
_____
_____
_____
_____
_____
_____
_____
_____
_____
_____
_____
_____
_____
_____
_____
_____
_____
_____
_____
_____
_____
_____
_____

DAY 19

TESTIMONY

READING: Psalm 71:16

A testimony is any real-life experience that takes an unpredictable turn. An example can be a shooting going on in a neighborhood and a family hasn't been shot at or unbearable pressure when several bills are due at one time and the individual trust God while He works it out. When a person is faced with any of these scenarios, how will he or she react? How does God show His ability to provide if one lacks nothing?

Therefore, a testimony is an opportunity that God can use to reveal who He is. An opportunity to see how much a person trusts and rely on God. A psalmist said, "I will go in the strength of the Lord God: I will make mention of thy righteousness, even of thine only" (Psalm 71:16, KJV). The psalmist acknowledges the might and strength of the Lord. He proclaims how he will face whatever comes his way and keep his thoughts on the righteousness of God which will give the assurance that all is well and going to be well.

Prayer: *Heavenly Father,*

When we experience the test in our lives help us to react the same as the psalmist with peace and confidence. AMEN

Reflection- Can circumstances or experiences that one endure reveal the power of God?

DAY 20

UNJUST

READING: 2 Timothy 2:15

The word *unjust* gives off the impression that something is wicked and not righteous; impure and unclean. But, in regards to this scripture the author which is Paul states that the Word of God will not be shaken and that there are two inscriptions known as "this seal," which is obedience and departing from iniquity, "nevertheless the foundation of God standeth sure, having this seal, the Lord knoweth them that are His. And, let everyone that nameth the name of Christ depart from iniquity" (2 Tim. 2:19, KJV).

The Word of God is dominant to the believers, which are the children of God. He knows us by name and wants us not to walk after the world's practices, but after His will. God knows that we live in a world where evil and unjust behavior is everywhere, but this doesn't give believers the permission to do what is wrong and blame the world. It's true that we all live in an imperfect world, but we serve a God that surpasses all sins and imperfections.

Prayer: *Heavenly Father,*

As we close to an end of this book, let us remember to stay pure and righteous like thee. AMEN

Reflection- Why is it so important to study the Word of God?

DAY 21

VAIN

READING: Psalm 127:1

Whenever an act or word is given in *vain* it can come out as conceited or be worthless without any value. Since the word vain is an adjective it has several different definitions. The one out of the list of many that will be use is the definition being of no value, importance, or any significance. This is what the Psalmist meant, when a church is built in vain and not have the presence of God inside; the building is just an exterior without the presence of life, "except the Lord build the house, they labour in vain that build it: except the Lord keep the city, the watchman waketh but in vain" (Psalm 127:1, KJV).

In other words, unless God is in the middle of it or the priority, the building doesn't have anything; no importance or meaning.

Prayer: *Heavenly Father,*

We ask that we may not show vain in worship, but value in everything that contains Thee. AMEN

Reflection- How can a person avoid living in vain?

DAY 22

WORSHIP

READING: Psalm 95:1

What does the word *worship* means? The first thought that may come to mind is praise, music, and a joyful noise. Another thought may be singing and songs. When it comes to worship all of the above are great and true, but *real* worship comes from *submission* and *self-identity*. The reason why *submission* is chosen is because one should want to surrender to God completely. This is how one can truly experience the might and power of God.

Next, is *self-identity*. The reason why *self-identity* is chosen is because one will have to examine themselves and accept His presence. When one combines the submission with the self-identity approach than the praise, music, singing, and songs will all come together to create "worship," which is the only response that believers have to thank God, "o come, let us sing unto the Lord: let us make a joyful noise to the rock of our salvation" (Psalm 95:1, KJV). When worship is present, so is the presence of God.

Prayer: *Heavenly Father,*

We pray and ask that our worship be true and real. AMEN

Reflection- Give an example of true worship and explain what that means to you.

DAY 23

YOUTH

READING: 1 Timothy 4:12

The youths today are overlooked and eager to grow up. Those that are twelve want to be twenty and the twenty year olds want to forget about guidance and throw away any morals or respect given to them. Youths should be flourishing, achieving goals, and following their dreams--- not young and pregnant, dropping out of school or doing other things, which is something that much prayer could prevent from happening. The youths are incredible and can do anything they put their minds too.

According to scripture, the Apostle Paul encouraged Timothy when he was a young man to, "let no man despise thy youth but be thou an example of the believers, in word, in conversation, in charity, in spirit, in faith, in purity" (1 Tim. 4:12, KJV). He reminded Timothy that he was a leader and one that could have great influence among his peers and others. Paul told Timothy to not allow those that were older to *despise* him, which meant to be of a negative state of mind, but instead be "an example" of how a youth should be and conduct themselves around other believers.

Prayer: *Heavenly Father,*

Please continue to protect and guide the youths to be the best they can be. AMEN

Reflection- Do you believe that a youth can lead a nation or a minor group?

DAY 24

ZEAL

READING: Psalm 71:23

Being zealous or having a zeal is being excited and estatic about the Lord. It is having a drive, the motivation to want to do more and see more. When zeal is in effect, the person knows what to use or apply to the fire to keep the flames going. For the psalmist said, "my lips will shout for joy when I sing praise to you--I whom you have delivered" (Psalm 71:23, KJV).

Through zeal, the psalmist said, "his lips will shout for joy" meaning the instrument will be the mouth that is used to give praise unto the Lord. The reason why the psalmist will praise the Lord is because the Lord has delievered him from life's turmoil and replace it with His joy. This would encourage anyone to want to thank God with gladness and much happiness. The zeal that one express comes from the presence of God and what He is able to do.

We do serve a good God and a God that can do exceedingly and abundantly!!

Prayer: *Heavenly Father,*

We thank you for the joy that YOU provide and so graciously give! Thank you!!

Reflection- Can the zeal of God be given to anyone or just believers?

The Holy Bible: King James Version. Thomas Nelson, 2004.

EPILOGUE

*(Special Words from the **Author**)*

While reading this devotional, I pray that all were encouraged and inspired to build an intimate relationship with God, our Creator. Through these mere pages, I hope many were able to express how they felt and how the chapters spoke volume to their mind, heart, and Spirit. God is amazing and loves us all unconditionally. In Him we all can be ourselves and love the individual that God created us to be. Thank you all so very much for the support and may God continue to bless you all on your journey.

-Chrystal V. Hollins

www.ingramcontent.com/pod-product-compliance
Ingram Content Group UK Ltd.
Pitfield, Milton Keynes, MK11 3LW, UK
UKHW022217230426
12048UKWH00016BA/902